Taken

poems by

Sarah Van Arsdale

Finishing Line Press
Georgetown, Kentucky

Taken

Copyright © 2021 by Sarah Van Arsdale
ISBN 978-1-64662-657-1 First Edition
All rights reserved under International and Pan-American Copyright Conventions. No part of this book may be reproduced in any manner whatsoever without written permission from the publisher, except in the case of brief quotations embodied in critical articles and reviews.

ACKNOWLEDGMENTS

Grateful acknowledgment is made to the editors of the following publications where original poems were first published:

Another Chicago Magazine: "Tulip Heart"
Clockhouse: "And I Was A Girl"
Los Siete Pecados: "What the Heart Wants" (in Spanish, translated by Maria Luisa Baragli)
The New Guard: "Taken" (finalist, New Guard Poetry Contest)
New Millennium Writings, "Taken" and "Undertow"
Transition: Poems in the Aftermath, "Ethics"

"Tulip Heart" is in the form of a Golden Shovel, using a line from Gwendolyn Brooks' "Second Sermon on the Warpland" to make up the end words of the lines.

Publisher: Leah Huete de Maines
Editor: Christen Kincaid
Cover Art: Raúl Soruco
Author Photo: Peter Bricklebank
Cover Design: Elizabeth Maines McCleavy

Order online: www.finishinglinepress.com
also available on amazon.com

Author inquiries and mail orders:
Finishing Line Press
PO Box 1626
Georgetown, Kentucky 40324
USA

Table of Contents

Taken 1

Ethics 3

Interstices 5

Guardian 6

Talisman 7

Confirmed 9

What the Heart Wants 10

The Thread, April, 2020 13

The Good Germans 14

The New World of Abstraction 16

And I Was a Girl 23

Undertow 24

After the Rain 25

Tulip Heart 26

Passover 27

In memory of my grandmother,
Virginia Allen Williamson,
and
my first poetry teacher: my mother,
Nancy Williamson Van Arsdale

Taken

The video of the girls
abducted from their dormitory
······a spare concrete square
······in dusty, far-off Nigeria
will begin in seven seconds.

While I wait, a white man on the screen
runs water from a hose
into a blue plastic pool.
It's the start of summer in America.
He makes a joke about his daughter:
how they can't communicate.
He's buying her a new cell phone.

In the video, the camera pans the girls
massed grey and black.
They are reciting words without apparent feeling.
There are so many of them, their shrouds so dark
that they blur into a single breathing animal.

My needs
are so easily satisfied
sometimes I feel I'm disappearing.

I once was a girl, alone on a Greyhound bus
heading back to my boarding school
where no one was watching.
Classes were held in a reformed barn.
Smoking was allowed in the old milking room,
concrete-walled, stinking, freezing in winter.
We huddled there, child-refugees from the wrecks of our families,
and at night, found our way to one bed or another,
dragging our broken hearts.

I navigated the 1970s Port Authority
weaving among tight-skirted, beaten-looking women
and men who sized me up as if I were hanging in a butcher's window.
I was careful to keep my face expressionless as a penny.
Then boarded another bus,
which sailed out into Jersey
where I paced the farmhouse kitchen,
the upstairs rooms echoing.
Everyone else had gone: my mother to her new apartment,
my father to his still-secret, better family.
Only the house remained,
the stained-glass window my father made,
my mother's fragrance lingering in her bedroom,
the books still on the shelves,
the willow tree weeping its branches to the wet, wet, grass.
Like a nuclear disaster
where the buildings are intact
but all the people are gone.

I could so easily have been taken.

But I wasn't, and now,
at last, someone is waiting for me,
wondering where I am and when I'll be home.

And the moon rose
a hammered silver disc
over the baobob tree.

Ethics

In a future I cannot imagine
will we say to each other,
*remember that afternoon,
that thing with the ethics committee,
was that when everything changed?*

Will we say,
was that before the inauguration?
and puzzle it out, tethering from Christmas
to Joan's party on New Year's Day?

*yes, it was early in January
yes, it was between the election
and the inauguration*

Will we say,
*remember, we drove up to the Catskills
it was raining
and we stopped for gas
and I bought a Times because the headline
was so alarming?*

We kept driving north on the Taconic
and it was that stasis
between late fall and true winter:
raining, but just after Hopewell Junction
the pond that forms there between the northbound
and the southbound lanes
was frozen over with a skin of ice
and the desperate trees, bare of leaves
scratched against the fog-heavy sky
and the apron of woods
banking up from the Parkway
lay littered with leafmeal
and patches of early snow.

Will we remember this afternoon,
the rain, the *Times* tossed into the back seat,
arriving at last, the clumps of snow
heaped by the trunks of the trees,
the warm purr of the furnace,
the roses resting, wrapped
against the coming freeze?

Interstices

Between the testimony and the truth
between the flushed face and the fire
between the measured and the meek
between the laughter and the lust
between the impossible and the imbecile
between the rage and the redundancy
between the woman and the war
between the pledge and the persistence
between the victim and the victor
between the silence and the semaphore
between the speaker and the spine
between the harangue and the hand
between the member and the mouth
between the adolescent and the adulterer
between the powerful and the powered
between the female and the fern
between the accuser and the accurate
between the maverick and the maimed
between the sniffle and the sty
between the accursed and the acclaimed
between the reddened and the risen
between the commiseration and the calm
between the beastly and the balm
between the strident and the struck
between the taken and the took
between the weighted and the weight

between his lying and her laid
       on that bed, in that room, in that memory.

Guardian

Before it was over, I knew I'd break his heart, and he'd break
mine. I was bound to disappoint him, even as I learned
the ropy, unfamiliar Spanish words: *asilo, pandilla, refugio.*

What could I guard him against? What real refuge
is there for a boy who's run without a break
across rivers, deserts, all the way through Mexico? I learned

his map, found the Guatemalan highlands, learned
what *pandilla* meant. It meant he needed refuge
from the gangs. It meant his brother's knees were broken.

Of course he'd had to run north, alone. In my broken
Spanish, I told him about the places of refuge
in our city. I told him where he could learn

English, where he might get work. I learned
he didn't even have an i.d. from Guatemala; this broke
my fantasy that I could save him, even with the refuge

offered by our ad-hoc group. What refuge
is this for a boy? A cot in the basement of the church. I learned
so much in those six months, and then he broke

away. I loved him, can't you see? He broke
my heart, surely as I broke his. I've learned
from this, that I can't expect anyone to be my refuge,

or my refugee. I wanted to claim him for my own.
I'm learning again how a heart can break.

Talisman

The night before I turned twelve
I was put on a plane
filled with strangers.
I wore a tag: *Unaccompanied Minor.*
I had a window seat
and as we sailed over the Atlantic
I looked down the wing
at the little light blinking there
and I thought my new word: *talisman,*
knowing the red light looked tiny
but was probably huge.

That's perspective, my mother had said,
as if this trip were necessary,
as if I was fleeing some grave danger,
and maybe I was,
my family's fissure cracking open at last
and me, alone on this flight,
both a wedge and a shim.

It was a *great opportunity!*
I was *going abroad!*
My birthday the same
as the Queen Mother's
and there would be fireworks,
and I'd never forget
how I turned twelve.

We had family in London
whom I'd never met.
I saw Buckingham Palace
and the Tower of London.
I rode a double-decker bus.
And on the living room sofa
while his parents were out,
my cousin, fifteen,

roamed his hands all over me
looking for something
that wasn't yet there,
while I waited, frozen,
afraid even to breathe.

And now,
all over the world
seas are filling with boats
tumbling up shore to shore,
pushed back to the surf,
children grasping the gunwales.

But I went home
and there was a banner my father had made
Welcome Home World Traveler
and my favorite
Black Forest Cake.

The day I turned twelve
the bells rang all over London
for the birthday of the mother of the queen.

Confirmed

We knew it would be bad, but even knowing man
and men we never would have guessed:
the senators, their gavels and their hands,
the fingers creeping underneath your dress.

The robes of justice with their tuck and blow
in winds of Washington's white air;
his thighs move, deliberate and slow
as he ascends the wide, bright marble stair.

Nightmare's stench; the paralytic fear;
the footfall coming closer on the stair;
the gut-churn at the day's news drawing near;
the things you say, the things you do not dare.

No longer slouching toward a Bethlehem that's burned,
his head held high, the shoulders squared: confirmed.

What the Heart Wants

> *The heart wants what it wants—*
> *or else it does not care.* —Emily Dickinson

Was it really greed, when, for years, we didn't know?
and got our tickets for France or Mexico or Spain,
the planes' contrails cottoning above the earth,
which appeared so perfectly blue and green,
so particular and small from way up high.

And later, when we knew, but said that there
was nothing we could do, was that greed, too?
We meant no harm. For years, we shrugged,
and whined about the coming heat and rain.
But if asked we would have denied
that greed was at the heart of what we were.
We only wanted what we had,
and just a little more.

We knew, in some larger sense, that everything we did
reverberated, blowing on the gathering winds
to other places,
imagined far-off farmlands
and dusty villages with goats,
foreign to us in their unfamiliar need.

But, calibrated for differences in income and priorities,
we had needs, too.
The stores were flooded with such a surfeit
of pretty tableware, blue glass bottles, percale sheets,
coats suited for winter, spring or fall,
and all that gear: backpacks and canoes,
hiking sticks, the tackle and the trim,
a spade for planting bulbs,
or for burying the ashes of our dead,
gauzy yellow curtains for the living room,
lace up boots, necklaces of polished stone,
all of it flown right to our doorsteps
from China, India, Peru.

And if it was greed, wasn't it her opposite,
generosity, too?
The polished wooden bowl for the wedding of a niece,
a flight to visit family in L.A.,
new novels by our friends,
which then we gave to other friends.
A first car for a son.

And look: what's more generous than this?
Easter baskets for the children of the refugees
sheltered in the church, filled
with green grass of cellophane,
chocolate eggs wrapped in foil.

And it wasn't luxury—at least, not to us—
we weren't shopping at Neiman Marcus
or buying Hermés scarves.
(Except that summer,
I bought that bag from Coach,
bright Kelly green,
as incentive to keep the job
I felt oppressive for another year.)

We were good, too, throughout it all,
guarding immigrants when the flood of human suffering
crowded to our borders,
giving money to the rescue groups
for the latest hurricane or flood.

We cared so much, sometimes it made us cry.

And, soon enough, we knew.
The goods we bought were taking something
from someone else, and isn't that what greed means?
Taking more than your fair share
when someone else doesn't have enough.

We demonstrated in the streets,
demanding that something must be done,
and we bought our many things
and took our groceries home in plastic bags,
and let our faucets and our summer hoses run.

We were texting one another on our phones
—made of cobalt, aluminum, and tin
mined by children in Congo and Brazil—
but we had to have them:
our imagination had expired
and the world was collapsing around us,
the wrecked procession of refugees
holding fast to the tops of trains
or floating through salty waves from Syria to Greece,
the wind picking up
the rains pelting our windows.

We needed—
the heart wants what it wants—or else it does not care—

a world safe from cyclones and the rising seas—

—and how I loved that jacket I bought
and didn't need, navy blue, prickled with delicate
pink and white blossoms,
so perfect for this, one of the last real springs.

The Thread, April, 2020

I wake each night at three or sometimes four
shadows stitching to the ceiling and the wall
a net to hold my nightmares and my dreams
a hammock for the bodies of the dead.

Stilled light tilts from the silent street.
I rise, and thread from room to room.
Outside, the darkened garden sleeps and swoons
as if anesthetized.

Now that we've finally arrived,
it's not the surging firestorm or flood
here, where catastrophe meets spring.
Mute the day, more muted is the night

pierced only by the stars
and by the sirens' *who who who*

The Good Germans
for Constance Bond

Did it start very small?
Did it seem inconsequential?
Did they even, at times, laugh about it?

Did they hear the news on the radio?
Was the signal scratchy?
Did they switch the radio off in frustration?

Did they laugh at his peculiar little mustache?
Did they pour coffee into a white ceramic cup?
Did they look in on their neighbor
the elderly Jew whose wife was ill?
Did they make love in the twilight?

Did they let the cat in
gold morning sun
aghast against the building opposite?
Did they read novels at night?
Did they no longer notice the church bells?
Did they eat a hearty dinner?
Were they occupied with their children?
Did they follow the latest fashions of dress?
Did they startle at sudden noises?
Did they say that maybe
it wouldn't as bad as they feared?

Did they sit together at a wooden table
listening to a speech on the radio
just as we do, palms pressed to the
solid surface of the wood,
wood that was cut from trees
in a black forest?

Did one of them say, "would you like more coffee"
and the other answer, "yes"
too stunned to say
anything more?

Were they writing poems?
Were they eating bread and jam?
Were they making summer plans?
Were they thinking of us, a future
where it would never happen again?

The New World of Abstraction

I.

Suddenly, everything was abstract:
the significance of things; their signifiers.
A buzzing blue haze
emitting from our palms
as we stumbled toward each other.
Stumbled toward, but missed.

II.

You'd think we would whisper our secrets
into the palms of our hands
the susurration of voices
a cooing to the blue light.

But we spoke loudly into the air
the shimmer in our palms
the color of anxiety itself
calling into the air, desperate,
>   *can you hear me*
>   *can you hear me*
>   *can you hear me now?*

III.

Can you hear me?
I've something that I've got to say
and it's trapped inside my burning brain.
It wakes me, two or three a.m.
when the city's hushed and the date palms
whistle in the night wind
and the lonely call of the underwood
and the pleading bark of the dog penned in.

It wakes me nearly every night
as if I've drunk too much
and now I'm up and sweating,
regretful, sore with dancing,
like when I was young and all the world
was a different and less abstracted place.

IV.

It fit into my palm
like that smooth black stone I found on Whidbey Island
shot through with a bolt of white.
Someone told me I could toss that stone
over my shoulder into Puget Sound
and my wish would come true.

Like that stone, my thing
felt as if it was made just for me,
but really, it was just like all the others.

Once, I was walking in the woods
and mine was in the pocket of my jacket
my jacket was open and it swung heavily
side to side with the weight
of my device, and my arms
were swinging up and down.

The day was big and brilliantly blue
my pocketed device kept knocking against my hand
and later, when we got to the beach,
I saw my wrist was bruised
a purple-yellow blossom
the color of butterflies' wings
and there, before me, the sea.

V.

We thought a lot about the sea.
We used to go there, but now there
were boats, insufficient boats
crowded with children and their adults.
We thought of ourselves as ordinary Americans,
and we thought a lot about the sea,
that place we went to when we were young,
a red and white cooler with sandwiches on ice,
how hot the sand was under our feet
how quickly it cooled as the sun went down.

We saw photographs of people we called "refugees"
the very word reducing them to language
when really they were this:
a callous on the palm breaking open.

VI.

We were sitting together
in rows, as if in a temple
one of those early ones
like the one I saw in the desert
at the Dead Sea,

but unlike that; not on benches
nautilused for prayer,
but in individual seats
and we were there in order to be someplace else;
we were moving from one place
on our planet to another.

We all sat together, hundreds of us at a time
but there was little human conversation,
just a steady thrumming sound,
an anesthetic stillness
as we began our descent.

Someone laughed;
it seemed a sound we hadn't heard in years.

VII.

We weren't talking; we were looking
at the bright square of light.
We each had our own,
we called it a screen,
but it was unlike a screen
because a screen is a garden hedge
 —*that burning scent of boxwood,
blue and green island summer*—
or a screen is dignified, rice paper and sweet rosewood
silk edge of a kimono disappearing

VIII.

We did it willingly.

IX.

We lined up, and walked into a machine
that could photograph us
as we are in the mornings, rising from sleep,
or as we are at night, in our beds
a lover's fingertip running along our collarbone.

We lifted our arms
and held our breath
as if in naked surrender.

X.

Increasingly, we were afraid,
and soon *have a nice day,*
(that yellow smiley-face from the 1980s)
was replaced with *have a safe day,*
as if every day was a territory
fuming with danger.

XI.

We had everything, and still we wanted more.

XII.

There were cameras everywhere: on street corners,
in elevators, over the dairy products in the market.
We knew we were under surveillance
but we forgot
and then, later, we didn't care.

XIII.

There was a lot of sleeplessness,
and we talked about sleep
—*a good night's sleep*—
as if it were something from the lost country
of our grandmothers,

who would say it was all we needed,
smoothing our hair back
wiping tears from our cheeks
with the back of a papery hand.

XIV.

Even at the doctor's office
there was a tiny camera
the cheerful clerk saying
take a step back
like that old joke
about the couple at the Grand Canyon,
the man who wanted to off his wife.
Take a step back,
and we did, not looking to see
the cliff behind us.

We were concerned about how we looked
for the photograph
and how long we'd have to wait.

XV.

We knew and said we didn't know
dark children were coughing in the night,
fevered, exhausted, afraid,
making possible our finger-taps
on the tiny, bright-lit sheet of glass.

While we walked upright, searching,
looking down into our palms,
children scrabbled deep into the earth
digging child-fingers into rocky dirt.

They held their breath to find
a vein of silica, thin as the remembered
strands of their mother's hair.

We knew the children did this
just for us—as children will—
they held out their hands,
palms up, displayed for pay and praise.

Then told to go back in again,
so we could send the messages
that seemed so important to us
at the time:

yes, I can meet at ten.
I like that place, too.
I'm here. Where are you?

And I Was a Girl

And I was a girl—fourteen? fifteen?—
alone on a Greyhound bus
traveling deep into the December night.
The lank-haired stranger beside me offering a cigarette,
then his hand on my leg, and then
almost everything.

When he got out—Brattleboro? Springfield?—
I was shaky with sex
My stomach in a churn and thud
and the bus curved
back onto the highway.

I pressed my face to the window
snow-ice ticking on the glass
the tobacco flats of Massachusetts
the houses of Connecticut
and finally the city
in its huge dimensions.

I had no idea then that I'd live this long.
Long enough
to see this desert lake,
the great dusting alkaline mist rising in huge sweeping gusts
and the dusky barn swallows creasing the air
their burnished bellies brushed with new Western light
as if lit from within
above the long meadow grasses.

I didn't know then the weight and the size
of my own will to survive.

The world was waiting for me—
birds, desire,
salt, fire, and flare—
as I despaired.

Undertow

The year my mother died,
hospital bed in her living room,
I flew to Puerto Rico with a lover
but even at the time I knew
it wouldn't last; she was afraid
of everything: the dark-skinned people
we met on the road
the volatility of Spanish.
She had never learned to swim
and stood on shore
while I dove into the thudding breakers,
then swam out to the sucking undertow,
pulling me farther than I'd wanted to go,
toward the coral reef
where seaweed tangled
around my legs and feet.

Not strong enough to fight the tide,
I swam, I rested, swam again,
tried to get back to the shore
and still was pulled away, not toward.
With just breath enough I lofted up,
arms flagging overhead, signaling to my lover
help, help, but she didn't understand
and thought I was waving in joy
at the sea and sky.

Sometimes it comes back to me,
that terrifying tide,
the sickening roil of the waves,
how easy it would have been
to slip beneath the shimmer of the sea.
What a struggle it can be to die.
How difficult it is to love someone.
How easy to misread a cry.

After the Rain

The river a silvery sheet of isinglass,
sheening silk the palest bluest grey:
mica, fish scales, my mother's eyes in her final days.

Over it all, the air still filled with mist,
the sky above a shattered slice of blue,
as if there really is another world above our world below.

In the park, the silver-wrench song of a warbler
tears the air and sears my heart with the spring-light
hope I wish that I could feel.

Tulip Heart

On your desk, a vase of tulips, yellow-red. This
curved and straight-stemmed colorcluster is
the force of life and beauty against the
grey, against the day's news, coming with its urgency:
the expected vote in Washington. But the tulips insist: *Live!*
and go on, even as they're dying too. And
you know the morning paper still awaits. But have
your coffee in your ceramic cup, the one your
mother made, wheel spinning underneath her feet. There's blooming
here, the lovely tulips' lovely line, green stems in
the watery glass, and ahead of you the
whole suffering day, the legislators' noise
about to shatter the world, but this is the stuff of
life, this is what it is to be awake. The
way you survive is to carry your tulip heart into the whirlwind.

Passover

We step into the Sea of Reeds
the stones knuckling our bare feet
seawater brindling our dusty legs.
Clutching our parcels of food, the babies,
a goatskin sack holding the bones of the dead.

You reach for my hand,
but I'm lofting someone's infant
over my head
out of the water's treacherous reach.

Behind us, across the desert pan,
the dusty ruckus of Pharaoh's horses.

The ribboning current
sluices around my hips,
now circling my waist,
my skirt ballooning with seastuff,
as I lift the infant higher,
the water now at my chest.

With your free arm
you reach beneath my shoulder
pulling me up toward the high, blue sky.

None of us knows what's on the other side
we're all at sea here
in the beautiful, mortal world
not knowing if the waters will part
or what's approaching from behind
how long it will take
or what relief may lie ahead.

Additional Acknowledgments

Thanks to the poets who have accompanied, encouraged, taught and inspired me: Bill Myer; Susan Stinson; Mark Doty, Alice Fulton, Pattiann Rogers, Eloise Klein Healy and Maura MacNeil at Vermont College; Molly Peacock; Rick Hilles; Elaine Sexton; Cornelius Eady; Rachel Hadas; Michael Broder; Alison Prine; David Groff, Janlori Goldman, Elisabeth Frost, Robin Messing, Dana Krugle, and Cris Beam; Ana Maria Spagna, Carol Potter, Dan Belm, Victoria Chang and my other colleagues at Antioch University; Sam Perkins, Joan Greenbaum, Kate Hogan, Barbara Blatner, Abby Beshkin, and everyone who has been a part of the BLOOM reading series. Se agradece profundamente a Raúl y Lina Soruco, por la imagen de la portada, y por su entusiasmo por la vida y el arte.

Thanks also to the following artists' residencies: Playa, where the title poem and "And I Was a Girl" were written; The Ragdale Foundation, where "Confirmed" and "Interstices" were written, and The Ricci Road Residency, where "Guardian" was written, and where this manuscript was completed.

Deep thanks to my family for believing in my poetry, and to Peter Bricklebank for his illimitable ability to keep my spirits up and my blood pressure down; without him, this book would not be in your hands.

Sarah Van Arsdale is the author of the novels *Toward Amnesia,* (Riverhead, 1995), *Blue* (University of Tennessee Press), winner of the 2002 Peter Taylor Prize for the Novel, and *Grand Isle,* (2012, SUNY Press). Her most recent book of fiction, *In Case of Emergency, Break Glass*, a novella collection, came out in 2016 with Queen's Ferry Press. Her poetry, fiction, non-fiction and book reviews have appeared in magazines including *The Florida Review, Guernica, Bayou, The AWP Writers' Chronicle, Clockhouse,* and *The New Guard.* She is the creator of several short animated films. She is on the affiliate faculty in fiction writing in the Antioch/LA Low-residency MFA program.

www.ingramcontent.com/pod-product-compliance
Lightning Source LLC
LaVergne TN
LVHW041513070426
835507LV00012B/1548